WHISPERS BEYOND THE VEIL

Channeled Teachings Inspired by the Spirit World

AMY MAROHN

Sensorium Press

Whispers Beyond the Veil
by Amy Marohn

Channeled Teachings Inspired by the Spirit World

Copyright © 2025-2026 Sensorium Press

ISBNs:
979-8-9996146-1-2: Paperback
979-8-9996146-0-5: eBook
979-8-9996146-3-6: Journal paperback

TABLE OF CONTENTS

INTRODUCTION

By Amy Marohn

A Quiet Return to What Has Always Been

I did not set out to write a book. I set out to listen and to learn.

To sit quietly in the presence of Spirit. To become still enough—empty enough—to receive what longed to be spoken through me, not from me.

And in that quiet, she came.

A spiritual teacher of extraordinary soul depth stepped gently through the veil. Not with fanfare. Not with performance. But with presence. With elegance. With the unmistakable vibration of love that transcends death, and the clarity of a soul who had nothing to prove. Strangely, I did not know her during her time on earth, nor had I ever studied her work. I learned about her from a colleague at a recent conference during a trance healing exchange.

What followed was not a dictation, but a dialogue of the heart. A soul-to-soul transmission. Each teaching in this book emerged through that communion: in quiet moments of meditation, channeled conversations, automatic writing, and the mysterious space between dreaming and being awake which I've come to regard as Spirit's favorite threshold. Through her divine sacred energy, I encountered an essence that felt strangely familiar—like meeting someone you somehow already know.

From that encounter, her presence began to take root in my awareness—subtle at first, but increasingly undeniable. There was a spiritual resonance between us that bypassed logic. It was as if her essence knew where it would be welcomed, and I had unknowingly left the door ajar.

Why she chose me as a conduit, I do not fully know. Perhaps it was the stillness I had cultivated through years of listening. Perhaps it was the softness of my heart, or the fact that I had no expectations, no agenda, and no preoccupation about who she was. I was an empty vessel, unknown to anyone of importance, and untouched by the weight of reputation. Maybe that emptiness was the very thing that made room for her presence to pour in.

Or perhaps, on some deeper level, we had made an agreement long before this lifetime began. A soul contract. A shared intention to bring light in a time when many seek comfort and healing. I do not pretend to understand it fully. I only know that once she entered my awareness, a new kind of clarity came with her, the kind that doesn't shout but quietly changes everything.

Upon completion of this book, I spent many weeks deliberating over whether to reveal my source by name. I considered how her inner circle might feel about her energies transferring through me, an unknown in the world of mediumship. I also wondered if not disclosing her name would be – in any way - disrespectful to her legacy. Thus, I waited patiently for her guidance which came forth as follows "the value of what is shared is far more important than the source." So it is.

This book and its teachings are not meant to be read quickly but entered as one would a sacred space – softly, reverently, and with a listening heart. Each chapter holds a frequency, a message, a mirror containing truths best received in stillness.

And while this wisdom comes through a feminine voice of the spirit world, it is offered for the remembrance of your own voice.

This book isn't about her. And it isn't about me. It's about you.

It's about what's been calling you home.

About the gentle unraveling of everything you were told to be, so you can finally become who you are.

You will not find formulas here. You'll find resonance.

You will not find instructions. You'll find an invitation.

To soften.

To trust.

To feel.

To come back to the ancient, unshakable wisdom within you—the subtle nudge that's always been there tucked beneath the surface of your awareness.

This is a book about releasing the beliefs and agenda of the ego – yes, but more than that, it is a book about finding your way home.

Back to joy.

Back to integrity.

Back to humility, to clarity, to the quiet power of a life lived in alignment with soul.

If you're tired of striving, you're in the right place.

If you've grown weary of a performance-driven life, this book will meet you in your humanity.

And if you've forgotten who you are beneath all the roles, titles, and tasks—may these words help you remember.

What I have learned from this channeled experience is that Spirit doesn't come to impress—it comes to heal.

So may this book be a healing.

A balm.

A light in the darkness.

And may you experience what the Divine feminine voice of the spirit world has shown me through her unwavering presence:

You are not separate from Spirit.

You are Spirit, remembering itself.

May the blending of our energy be a warm welcome home.

WITH DEEPEST GRATITUDE

To Robbie Konikoff—who entered my life when I was fifteen years old, stepping into my parents' living room to hear a lost teenager's early compositions. With patience and humility, you listened to my clumsy melodies on a worn, untuned piano, and opened the doors of your recording studio—and your heart. You became more than a mentor. You became a guardian, wrapping me in grace during the most fragile years of my life. You taught me how to love and be loved unconditionally, how to live simply and honestly, and how to run a heart-centered business that nourishes people from the inside out. Music saved me. Your friendship transformed me.

To the late Jerry Starr—who directed nearly every musical theater performance of my youth and early adulthood. Thank you for your humor, warmth, and steadfast encouragement. You were the father figure every young artist longs for: generous, present, and uplifting. Your model of soulful leadership has shaped the way I hold space for others to this day.

To Stephanie DiCarlo—my junior high music teacher, who healed my wounded inner child and gently guided her into a safe and nourishing environment. Your countless hours of instruction, encouragement, and performance mentorship helped me find not just my voice, but my courage. Thank you for being a bright and steady light in those early years.

To all those I've had the pleasure of serving in my spiritual hypnotherapy, coaching and mediumship practice over the last decade. Thank you for trusting me, inspiring me and challenging me. I would not be where I am today, personally or professionally, had our paths not crossed. Your struggles, growth, and evolution laid the groundwork for my training path, workshop development, and everything I've written leading up to this first book.

To my beloved son, Reid—who, at the age of five, insisted he chose me as his mom. I believe we chose each other. You are the greatest gift of my lifetime. You are also the oldest soul I have ever known with an "other-worldly" intelligence, compassion and wisdom that takes my breath away and keeps me humble. I know you are here not only to walk with me, but to heal and guide me back to myself.

And to Wes—my partner, my anchor, my safe harbor. You are the only romantic partner or human in my life who has shown up for me with unwavering consistency. Your love, humor, loyalty, and humility have sustained me through my many health storms and life's unravelings. You held me when I could not hold myself. Your presence is a quiet miracle orchestrated by angels.

CHAPTER 1 – THE SACRED PRACTICE OF SITTING IN THE POWER

There is a subtle but unmistakable shift in the atmosphere when Spirit arrives.

A gentle stillness descends. The noise of the world softens. Time becomes irrelevant.

And if you listen closely enough, you may notice a slight ringing in your ear—or, as in my case, the feeling of floating in outer space—your consciousness suspended in the great expanse of all that is.

This is how she made her presence known to me. Not with grandeur or theatrics, but through sensory nuance. It was her invitation—one that beckoned me not only to listen, but to sit and remember.

What Is Sitting in the Power?

> *"Sitting in the power is not a technique. It is a devotion."*
> — Spirit World

It is the daily practice of quieting the mind, attuning to Spirit, and steeping yourself in the life force of the unseen. Unlike meditation, which often seeks calm or clarity, sitting in the power is about expansion. It's about plugging yourself directly into Source and allowing the natural energy of Spirit to infuse, recalibrate, and align you.

You are not visualizing.
You are not asking.
You are not scripting a manifestation list.
You are becoming.

In this state, the boundaries between the physical and non-physical blur.
You feel your auric field grow. Your thoughts slow down.
You begin to experience the presence of those who walk with you in Spirit—not as separate entities but as extensions of your own soul wisdom.

Why It Matters

Spirit was quick to point out that skipping this practice is like "darting into traffic without looking" or "showing up to a test completely unprepared." We wouldn't manage our daily lives this haphazardly, yet we do it spiritually all the time.

We scroll. We strive. We stuff ourselves with information, hoping that knowledge will substitute for connection. But the soul knows better. The soul wants alignment, not achievement. It wants devotion, not distraction.

Just as muscles atrophy when unused, so too do the spiritual faculties—clairvoyance, clairsentience, intuition, presence. These lie dormant until called upon. Sitting in the power exercises these inner instruments. It prepares the vessel.

The Maturity of Listening

> *"There comes a time when your prayers must*
> *evolve from asking to allowing."*
> *– Spirit World*

As spiritual seekers, we are conditioned to pray with requests, intentions, and goals. But the real power comes when we sit in reverent silence and simply ask: What would you have me know today? This is the hallmark of mature spiritual prayer.

We stop pleading and start listening.
We release egoic demands and soften into trust.
We surrender the timeline, the outcome, the specifics —
and allow our energy to align with what is best for all
souls involved, not just our human wants.

The reward? Presence. Alignment. Clarity. Guidance that doesn't have to shout because you've already become quiet enough to hear it.

Beyond Books and Gurus

> *"There is no speaker or book on Earth that can replace the wisdom of connecting with Spirit. None."* — *Spirit World*

You could spend a lifetime devouring spiritual texts and still never hear the whisper meant just for you. That whisper only comes in the quiet, in the power.

This is not to dismiss teachings or mentors, they have their sacred place. But Spirit must be your first and final authority. You must become the tuning fork.

Sitting in the power teaches you how to discern what resonates and what doesn't—not because someone told you, but because you feel it in your bones.

A Beginner's Guide to Sitting in the Power

Step-by-Step Practice:

1. Find a quiet place. Sit comfortably with your spine straight.
2. Close your eyes. Take a few deep, slow breaths.
3. Bring your awareness inward. Notice your heartbeat. Your breath. The space around you.
4. Imagine your inner light expanding from your chest, radiating gently outward.
5. Say silently: *"I attune to my soul and the power of Spirit."*
6. Allow yourself to simply be in that energy. No asking. No effort. Just presence.
7. After 5–10 minutes, slowly return. Ground yourself with breath or movement.

The Forgotten Path of Daily Devotion

In a world obsessed with optimization, quick wins, and instant downloads, it can feel outdated—even impractical—to sit in silence each day. But Spirit reminds us that the most inspired minds in history—scientists, mystics, poets, inventors—listened beyond the veil of the material world.

Some knew they were communing with Spirit. Others may have called it intuition or some kind of muse – something or someone that inspires creativity and ideas. But the source was the same: a higher intelligence flowing through a willing vessel.

Few humans reach the level of spiritual fluidity where they toggle seamlessly between dimensions. Fewer still marry the worlds without even realizing it. This is not just talent. It is discipline. It is practice. It is presence.

Journaling Prompts

1. What does it mean to me to be spiritually present? How does that feel in my body?
2. What distractions prevent me from connecting with my own inner power?
3. How do I typically pray? What would it look like to simply listen instead?
4. Have I ever experienced the presence of Spirit in stillness? If not, am I open to it?
5. What would it look like to prioritize this practice in my daily life?

Daily Self-Reflection Exercise: Staying Attuned to Spirit

Practice This Week:

- Choose a consistent time of day.
- Light a candle or set an intention.
- Start small by sitting in the power for 5–10 minutes, working your way up to 20 minutes, using the steps above.
- After each session, write one word or sentence about what you noticed or felt.

At the end of the week, reflect on the following:

- What changed in me?
- What felt difficult? What felt natural?
- How can I deepen this practice?

A Final Reflection

"Don't seek fireworks. Seek the flame. Let your presence be the prayer. Let your stillness be the invitation." – Spirit World

---

If you are reading this, consider yourself called. Spirit is not asking for your perfection—only your presence.

Start small. Five minutes. Ten. Sit with your eyes open or closed. Breathe. Notice. Feel. Let your consciousness rise.

And most of all, listen—not to the voice of your to-do list, your doubts, or your inner critic—but to the silence underneath. That is where Spirit waits. This is where power lives.

In sitting with your soul, you begin to know the self that Spirit already recognizes. You become not a seeker of Spirit, but a mirror of it.

CHAPTER 2 – LISTENING, NOT ASKING: REFRAMING THE ART OF PRAYER

There is a moment in every spiritual journey when the seeker realizes that the answers they long for are not "out there." Not in the next oracle card. Not in the next teacher. Not in the next manifestation journal prompt.

There is only one place left to go—inward. And that inward space is where true communion with Spirit begins.

But the challenge is this: we've been conditioned to treat Spirit like a cosmic vending machine. Insert prayer, expect delivery. Make a wish, wait for signs.

This is spiritual immaturity disguised as devotion.
True communion—true alignment—comes when we stop asking and start listening.

The Highest Form of Prayer

> *"Sitting in the power is the highest form of prayer," Spirit says.*
> *"It is not about seeking blessings — it is about becoming a blessing."*

Spirit doesn't mince words. Prayer, she reminds us, is not a list of requests. It is not a rehearsal of grievances. It is not a declaration of what we think we deserve.

Prayer, in its most potent and evolved form, is about quiet surrender. It is about entering a sacred stillness where our agendas fall away and our hearts open wide — not to get, but to receive.

And there is a difference.

- *To get* implies effort, striving, and entitlement.
- *To receive* requires only presence, trust, and openness.

Spirit likens this shift to moving from negotiation to reverence — from the vibration of "please give me" to the frequency of "I trust what you offer."

This is what Spirit calls spiritual maturity.

The Trouble with Asking

Why is asking problematic? Because asking often comes from ego—the part of us that believes it knows best.

We ask for what we think we need, based on what we currently understand. But our understanding is filtered—through trauma, through desire, through culture, through fear.

Spirit sees beyond this.

Spirit does not operate in straight lines or human logic. It operates in alignment.

If your desire is out of alignment with your soul's growth—or the growth of others—it will not come to pass in the way you expect.

This is not punishment. It's protection.

The spiritual path asks us to go deeper than desire. It asks us to pause before we ask, and instead say:

- "What would you have me know today?"
- "What would serve the highest good in this moment?"
- "How can I be of service to the unfolding?"

The Power of Listening

"The quality of your listening determines the quality of your life."
— Spirit World

When we begin to pray this way—not to speak, but to listen—everything begins to shift. Spirit no longer feels distant or reluctant.

Instead, it begins to speak… softly, symbolically, sometimes in silence itself.

Those who listen well live well—not because they are free from struggle, but because their struggles no longer derail them. They are anchored in divine timing, held by unseen hands, and guided by a Source that never withholds truth from the ready heart.

Trusting the Unseen Workings

---

*"There are a great many things that go on behind
the scenes of your life that unfold in the quiet."*
— Spirit World

Preparations you cannot see. Alignments you are not yet aware of. Interventions that reroute what would otherwise be painful detours. And all of this unfolds in the quiet.

We often dismiss these subtleties in our rush for certainty. We want fast answers. Fast results.

But Spirit is not bound by time—it is bound by truth. And truth requires readiness.

Spirit will never hand you something your soul isn't equipped to carry.

That's why so much of the work is internal:

- Learning how to trust the unfolding even when we don't understand it.
- Learning how to wait without collapsing.
- Learning how to say "yes" to what is, rather than trying to manifest what isn't.

Releasing the Bargaining Table

As you grow spiritually, you'll be asked to give up bargaining with Spirit.

That means:

- No more bartering your rituals for results.
- No more praying with ultimatums.
- No more saying "I'll do this if you give me that."

This kind of spiritual negotiation is a sign of misalignment. It places you in a transactional relationship with the Divine rather than a collaborative one.

Spirit already knows what you need — and more importantly, what you are here to become. When you release the need to control, you create space for Spirit to offer something better than what you imagined. Something more lasting. Something more sacred.

Journaling Prompts

1. How do I typically approach prayer or spiritual connection? Do I ask or do I listen?
2. What is one area of my life where I feel tempted to bargain with Spirit?
3. How might my spiritual life change if I stopped asking and started trusting?
4. What does spiritual maturity mean to me? Where have I seen it in my own journey?
5. Am I open to receiving something greater than what I asked for?

Self-Reflection Exercise: The Listening Prayer

Practice This Week:

- Choose a quiet space.
- Sit in the power for 10-20 minutes.
- Do not ask for anything. Instead, simply say inwardly: *"Spirit, what would you have me know today?"*
- Sit in silence. Notice what arises—thoughts, sensations, insights, or stillness.
- Afterward, write a brief reflection on what you experienced or received.

At the end of the week, review your journal:

- What themes or guidance appeared?
- Did anything shift in how you relate to Spirit?
- What would it look like to make this form of prayer a regular part of your life?

A Final Reflection

"To listen is to open your heart to love. To receive is to trust. And in that trust, your soul becomes available to miracles." — *Spirit World*

What if prayer wasn't a request, but an invitation? What if instead of asking Spirit to rearrange your life, you asked Spirit to readjust your lens? To help you see the beauty already in motion, the healing already underway, the synchronicities already dancing at the edge of your awareness?

This is not passive spirituality. This is powerful trust. It is the radical act of releasing ego in favor of soul. It is what allows the veil to thin and your higher knowing to rise.

This is what the spirit realm desires most: not your perfection, not your effort—just your presence, your openness, and your willingness to truly listen.

CHAPTER 3 – SPIRIT-LED VERSUS EGO-LED LIVING: FOLLOWING THE ORGANIC FLOW OF THE SOUL

"Replace the word spiritual with organic.
When something unfolds organically, without
force or manipulation, you are witnessing the hand
of Spirit." – Spirit World

There's something quiet and revolutionary about a life led by Spirit. It doesn't look particularly dramatic from the outside—no grand gestures, no shouting from rooftops. But when you're living it, everything feels different. Decisions land more softly. Timing feels more precise. Even the hard days carry a strange sort of grace.

That's because Spirit never pushes. It flows.

Spirit-led living feels like an "effortless yes." It moves without friction—not because life becomes easy, but because you're no longer swimming against the current. There's no internal war between what you know and what you're doing. You act when it feels right. You wait when you're meant to wait. You follow the quiet nudge instead of chasing the loud promise.

And often, it's only in hindsight that you realize something greater was carrying you all along.

The Effortless Yes

We don't always trust ease. Many of us were taught to believe that effort equals value—that if something comes without struggle, it must not be real. But this belief I had was challenged. She taught that ease, when aligned with depth, is one of Spirit's native languages.

She'd describe how a door would open unexpectedly, gracefully with precision—and how her only job was to recognize it and walk through. No forcing. No bargaining. Just noticing.

This doesn't mean Spirit bypasses difficulty. It means that when something is Spirit-led, even difficulty serves a deeper unfolding.

It's not passive. It requires acknowledgement and gentle movement.

It's not about waiting for life to happen to you. It's about participating in life's unfolding without pushing your agenda onto it.

The Subtle Ways Ego Imitates Spirit

Of course, ego doesn't always show up wearing red flags. More often, it dresses itself up in language that sounds wise. Responsible. Even spiritual.

It says, "Don't just sit there—do something." "Be realistic." "You can't let this happen to you."

At first glance, that seems sensible. But if you listen beneath the surface, you'll hear something else: fear, distrust and urgency.

Spirit called this the "fidgeting mind"—that restless impulse to keep tweaking our circumstances, as if one more adjustment to the outer world will finally quiet the storm within. It's like refreshing your inbox every few seconds, hoping peace will arrive as a new message. But it never does—because peace doesn't come from updates. It comes from stillness. From presence. From remembering who you are underneath the noise.

Ego thrives on movement. Spirit speaks through momentum. One reacts, the other reveals.

The difference is felt in the body. When ego is driving, you'll feel tight, frantic, unsure—despite having all the plans. When Spirit is leading, you may not have a clear path, but you'll feel rooted. There's an inner steadiness that whispers, "*Just take the next step.*" *The way will reveal itself.*

When Leadership Becomes Performance

She often spoke about the traps helpers and leaders fall into—especially when ego begins to hide behind service.

It may take the form of mediums striving for applause, healers clinging to certainty, leaders or teachers caught in performance. Not because they lacked devotion—but because their ego still needed proof that they were worthy.

"You're not here to save anyone," Spirit said. "You're here to walk beside them until they remember they were never lost."

That one concept held so much.

Leadership, real spiritual leadership, isn't about being impressive. It's about being available. It's about presence, not performance. Soul rather than style.

When you drop the need to prove, your energy becomes more porous. More grounded. People aren't drawn to your certainty—they're drawn to your sincerity.

And depth doesn't come from doing more. It comes from being more. More willing. More open. More attuned to what is quietly blooming underneath the minutia of daily life.

What Alignment Feels Like

"Your soul doesn't care about your five-year plan. It cares about who you're becoming." – Spirit World

Spirit said it best. When you're in alignment, things still go wrong—but you no longer collapse. You might wobble, but you don't lose your center.

It's like rowing a boat in a river that already knows where it's going. You still have to row—but you're not steering against the current anymore. You're part of something larger. Something intelligent.

You stop micromanaging miracles.

You stop forcing timing.

You stop treating peace like a reward you must earn.

Instead, you begin to trust the organic unfolding—the invisible architecture that Spirit has already set in motion.

Journaling Prompts

These reflections are not tasks to check off, they are quiet invitations to go deeper. Let your answers rise slowly. Let them surprise you.

1. Where in my life am I striving to be impressive, rather than being authentic?
2. Am I listening for Spirit—or only reacting to pressure?
3. When was the last time something fell into place without effort? How did it feel?
4. What do I turn to when I feel spiritually disconnected? Does it bring me closer—or just keep me busy?
5. What solitary or creative practice brings me back to myself?

Self-Reflection Exercise: Releasing the Plan

This week, identify one area of your life where you've been clinging tightly to a plan—whether it's a decision, a relationship, or an outcome you're trying to force.

Instead of asking, "What should I do next?"

Ask: *"What is Spirit already doing here?"*

Sit in the power—not to solve, but to soften. Don't try to figure it all out. Just listen.

At the end of the week, reflect:

- Did anything shift when I stopped managing and started listening?
- What became clearer when I allowed stillness to lead?

A Final Reflection

"Let Spirit pave the path. Then walk it. Don't just follow the light—become it.
— Spirit World

There is a rhythm to life that your soul already knows. It's not a schedule. It's not a checklist. It's not a performance.

It's an invitation.

An invitation to trust what you cannot yet see. To rest in timing that may not feel convenient but is always divine.

Flow is not passivity—it is participation with the deeper current.

It is the willingness to be led. To be moved. To be changed from the inside out.

CHAPTER 4 – THE MEDIUM WITHIN US ALL: AWAKENING YOUR INTUITIVE WISDOM AND HEALING PRESENCE

"Let the message pass through your heart. Let the presence of Spirit speak through your energy, not just your words. If the person leaves feeling more loved, more seen, and more whole—you have done the work."
— Spirit World

There is a kind of mediumship that doesn't require a platform, an audience, or even a label. It doesn't depend on how many spirit communicators you can name or how often you get "evidence." It lives, instead, in the quiet moments when love finds a voice through you.

Spirit believes that mediumship was not the possession of the few—it is the inheritance of the many. "You are all sensitive to Spirit," she said. "The question is not *if* you can connect. The question is, *will* you allow it to change you?"

Mediumship isn't only about bringing through messages from beyond. It's about being a message in the here and now. It's about letting your presence become a conduit for something higher—something healing, truthful, and whole.

Mediumship Is Your Birthright

You don't need a stage to serve Spirit.

For too long, the word *medium* has carried a sense of exclusivity, something reserved for those with unusual gifts or inherited abilities. But the Spirit World shattered that illusion and reminded me that mediumship begins the moment we live in alignment with love.

To be a medium, in the truest sense, is to be sensitive to the sacred.

- When you sit beside someone in grief without trying to fix them—just being there, heart open—you are serving Spirit.
- When you follow an inner nudge to reach out to someone, not knowing why, only to hear, "I really needed this"—you are already acting as a medium.
- When your energy brings calm, your words bring light, your eyes soften and communicate nonjudgment—you are delivering more than comfort. You are delivering connection.

You don't have to be known. You don't have to be right. You only must be present.

Resonance Over Performance: Why Some Messages Heal and Others Fall Flat

---

"Two singers can hit the same note, but only one will bring tears to your eyes."
— Spirit World

There's a vast difference between saying something true and saying something that *lands*. Between offering facts and offering transformation.

One performs. The other becomes the sound.

This is the power of resonance. It's what makes a message healing rather than hollow. It's not about clever phrasing or perfect phrasing—it's about truth with energy behind it. Whether you're delivering a formal message or speaking gently to a friend, what matters most is not what you say, but *who* you are as you say it.

Presence is the power. Energy is the language. Resonance is the outcome.

Presence Over Protocol: The Heart of Healing Connection

Many spiritual seekers get caught up in the mechanics—opening their "clairs," reading symbols, mastering delivery. And while these tools are valuable, they are not the essence.

"You are not a microphone," Spirit said. "You are the music."

Technique may impress. But presence heals.

Healing does not flow from polished performance. It flows from grounded hearts, from those who have learned to sit in their own silence long enough to hear what others cannot yet receive. True connection cannot be forced through form—it must be offered through feeling.

The Power of Feeling: Clairsentience as a Gateway to Truth

Of all the intuitive faculties, Spirit most revered *clairsentience*—clear feeling.

Because when you feel with someone, not just for them, something changes. A bridge forms. A softness enters the room. Your presence becomes medicine.

Feeling is not weakness. It is a gift.

Spirit doesn't always speak in words, it moves through sensation, atmosphere, impression. When you allow yourself to feel deeply—without analyzing, without resisting—you become a sacred vessel. A carrier of comfort. A mirror for what is most divine.

You Are the Instrument

Your intuitive gifts don't live "out there." They live within *you*.

Your body is the channel. Your energy field is the canvas. Your awareness is the tuning fork.

When you are attuned, you create resonance. When you are caught in ego, you create noise.

She taught that four inner qualities keep your spiritual instrument in tune:

- *Presence:* Be here. Not in the future, not in performance.
- *Reverence:* Remember the sacredness of what you're doing.
- *Humility:* Let Spirit lead.
- *Honesty:* Say what you feel. Trust what you know — even when it surprises you.

It's not about being flashy. It's about being faithful to the vibration of your own soul.

From Messenger to Healer

Many intuitive practitioners aim for accuracy. And yes, validation matters. But it's not the whole story.

The question isn't "Was it right?"

The question is "Did it reach them?"

If your words leave someone feeling seen...

If your energy reminds them they are not alone...

If your presence helps them exhale something they didn't know they were holding...

Then you've done the deeper work.

That is spiritual service. Not to impress. But to hold. To witness. To offer something so real and human that the soul remembers what it came here to feel.

Your Unique Soul Tone

Every soul has a sound.

Your intuitive voice is shaped by your sincerity, your emotional range, your life story. It cannot be faked—and it should not be copied.

"Do not become a copy of someone else's voice," Spirit warned. "Become a clear amplifier of your own soul's resonance."

When your words come from truth, they ring differently. They carry weight. They vibrate. And it is that vibration that Spirit recognizes.

The work is not to mimic another's delivery. The work is to refine your own.

Redefining Mediumship: Walking with Spirit in Ordinary Life

What if mediumship were less about talking to Spirit—and more about walking *with* Spirit?

This reframes mediumship not just as a moment, but rather a *manner* or an *energy*.

- When you listen deeply to a child.
- When you show patience in traffic.
- When you choose compassion over cleverness.
- When you create beauty, tend to grief, speak truth with grace…

That, too, is mediumship.

Let go of the stage. Let go of the title. Ask instead: *Does Spirit move through my everyday life?* If the answer is yes, you are already doing the work.

Journaling Prompts

The Power of Resonance and Presence

1. When have you experienced a message that touched your soul, not just your mind?
2. Have you ever tried too hard to "get it right" in spiritual work? What changed when you focused on presence?
3. How do you personally define resonance? How is it different from accuracy?

Becoming an Instrument for Spirit

4. Do you see yourself as a vessel for healing or guidance?
5. What spiritual or emotional practices help keep you "in tune"?
6. Where do you feel dissonance in your life right now?

The Role of Feeling in Spiritual Connection

7. Are you comfortable letting emotion move through you during healing work?
8. What do you fear about being emotionally available in spiritual spaces?
9. Reflect on a time when your intuitive empathy helped someone. What shifted?

Honoring the Sacred in Everyday Connection

10. How do you recognize sacredness in daily life?
11. Where do reverence, humility, and honesty show up in your practice?
12. What would happen if you treated your daily life as a form of Spirit work?

Your Unique Tone and Voice

13. What does your soul "sound" like? (e.g., steady, playful, deep, light?)
14. Have you ever mimicked someone else's style? What did you learn from that experience?
15. What would it look like to more fully amplify your soul's tone?

Everyday Mediumship

16. Recall a recent time when you brought comfort to someone without trying.
17. Do you limit your spiritual identity to a formal setting?
18. Envision a day where Spirit works through your thoughts, words, and presence. What shifts?

A Final Reflection

Mediumship is not an event. It is a way of being.

It's not about the words you say—it's about the energy you carry. It's not about visibility. It's about vibration.

Every day, Spirit asks the same quiet question:

Can I move through you today?

And your answer doesn't have to be grand. It doesn't have to be formal.

It just has to be true.

When you hold someone in their pain, when you speak from a place of reverence, when your love becomes the message—*you are the medium.*

And that, Spirit reminds us, is the highest calling of all.

CHAPTER 5 – THE MOVING POWER: LISTENING THROUGH FLOW, CREATIVITY, AND PRESENCE

"The sacred is not a place. It is a presence. It moves through you when you create, when you serve, when you allow yourself to be part of something greater." – Spirit World

---

There's a quiet misunderstanding regarding spiritual connection that stillness must look like silence. Eyes closed. Hands resting. Incense lit. As if Spirit only visits when the room is dimmed and the breath is slow.

But Spirit—always the truth-teller—gently guided me away from that illusion. "You can be in the kitchen washing dishes and still be in the power," she said. "Spirit isn't waiting for you to be still. It's waiting for you to be *attuned*."

Stillness, in her view, isn't the absence of movement. It is the presence of receptivity. You could be dancing, gardening, folding laundry—and if your heart is open, Spirit can walk right in and sit beside you.

And so, we learn to listen differently. Not just with ears in silence, but with a body moving through life, fully present, fully available.

Spirit Moves With You

Stillness is a frequency, not a posture.

Many seekers believe they must sit cross-legged and silent to commune with Spirit. But She reminds us, "sitting in the power isn't about stillness. It's about receptivity."

And receptivity isn't confined to one shape. It doesn't belong only to meditation cushions or ceremonial rooms. It shows up in paint strokes. In music. In the rise and fall of your feet on the trail. It flows through the clatter of pots in the kitchen, the rhythm of breath while dancing, the hush between words as you write.

Stillness isn't a lack of movement. It's a presence that *moves with you*.

Expanding the Practice

Every moment can become a channel.

When She spoke about "sitting in the power," she wasn't speaking only about posture. She was speaking about presence.

It's about that sacred moment when your inner noise softens and you remember who you are—not a seeker trying to get it right, but a soul remembering *how to receive.*

This might happen when you walk alone under trees.

It might happen when you scribble in your journal without planning what will pour out.

It might come in a melody that seems to write itself, or in the rhythm of hands kneading dough while in a deep pensive state.

Even cleaning the floor can become a kind of prayer, if done with awareness.

"These are not distractions," She said. "They are doorways."

Beyond the Meditation Cushion

Let go of trying to do it "Right."

There is no gold star for perfect stillness. There is no divine checklist that scores you for posture or practice. But ego—clever thing that it is—will often try to turn spirituality into performance.

You don't need to be quiet to be open. You need to be present. Fully. Sincerely. Without pretense.

Whether you're sitting with closed eyes, laughing with your children, or weeping quietly in your car, if your heart is open—Spirit is already near.

She, in her no-nonsense way, called it out, "Spirit is not looking for your stillness. Spirit is looking for your resonance."

Creative Flow as Divine Channel

Your art Is your access point.

So many people dismiss their creativity as "just a hobby." Spirit sees it differently.

"Your art," she said, "is a form of mediumship."

A single lyric can lift despair. A stroke of color can unearth a memory. A poem scribbled on a notepad can stir something ancient in someone's soul. These aren't accidents. These are transmissions.

"Spirit weaves through your hands, your voice, your movement," She said. "It infuses your energetic imprint into everything you create."

When you let yourself enter that creative space—not to perform, but to connect—you become a channel. Not by trying harder, but by getting out of the way.

The Sacred Shift: From Doing to Being

It's easy to think spirituality is something you *do*. You go to the workshop. You pull the card. You light the candle.

"It's not about doing spiritual things," she said. "It's about *becoming* a spiritual presence."

Spiritual living is an internal state, not a behavior.

It's about how you move through the world. How you touch what's in front of you. Whether you're making tea, answering emails, or standing in line, the question is the same:

Are you present?

Are you receptive?

Are you willing to let Spirit move through this moment— even this one?

When the answer is yes, every act becomes prayer.

Living the Practice

Let Spirit meet you where you are.

You don't need to wait for the perfect moment to feel spiritual. Spirit doesn't live only in ceremony. It lives in the realness of your day.

Spirit encouraged creating what she referred to as a "Soulful Practice Menu"—a collection of small, personal rituals that reconnect you to your inner knowing:

- Walking with reverence
- Writing without an agenda
- Listening to music that softens your armor
- Cooking, cleaning, or creating with intention—not to complete a task, but to commune with life.

The form doesn't matter. Your presence does.

And above all, trust your own rhythm. You don't need to copy anyone else's path. Your breath, your movement, your energy are already sacred instruments. Let them guide you back to the presence that never left.

"Your power may be in motion. Trust it."

Journaling Prompts

The Power of Resonance and Presence

1. What does "stillness" mean to me? Where do I experience it most naturally?
2. Have I ever felt closer to Spirit while in motion or creating something?
3. What moments in my day feel like natural entry points to spiritual connection?

Creative Communion

4. What is one creative act I lose myself in? Could I treat it as sacred?
5. How does my energy shift when I am fully absorbed in creating or moving?
6. What intuitive insight have I received while doing something physical?

Trusting My Way In

7. Do I judge how I "should" be spiritual? Where did I learn that?
8. What does my unique soul rhythm look and feel like in daily life?
9. What might Spirit be saying to me through color, sound, or rhythm?

A Final Reflection

Power isn't always still. Sometimes it dances.

Sometimes it paints. Sometimes it walks barefoot through the grass with tears in its eyes. It sings. It stirs. It waits in the smallest moment of yes.

The sacred doesn't only arrive in hushed rooms. It shows up where you are—*if* you are willing to let it in. Spirit reminds us: "Stop worrying about whether you're doing it right. Start listening. Start opening. Start trusting."

Stillness isn't the goal. *Presence* is.

And presence doesn't require you to stop moving.

It only asks you to stop hiding.

CHAPTER 6 – WISDOM BEYOND KNOWLEDGE: WHY THE MIND ALONE CAN'T LEAD THE SOUL

"We are obsessed with knowledge, often mistaking it for intelligence.
But true wisdom cannot be regurgitated. It must be received."
– Spirit World

We live in an age of information, where knowledge is praised, collected, shared—and often mistaken for spiritual depth. But Spirit reminds us, just because something is *known* doesn't mean it's *understood*. True wisdom doesn't come from reciting what others have said. It arrives through surrender, silence, and soul-level recognition.

The mind, while helpful, is not the captain of the soul. It's the compass—but not the wind. And when we let wisdom rise through intuition rather than intellect, we don't just gather ideas—we allow ourselves to be *changed*.

Knowledge Versus Wisdom

"Information fills the mind. Wisdom shapes the soul."
— Spirit World

There's a vast difference between being informed and being transformed.

We live in a world that praises accumulation—collecting facts, quoting experts, chasing certifications. There's nothing wrong with education, but without integration, knowledge remains surface level. It dances on the surface but never sinks into the current that transforms.

She explains that real spiritual growth doesn't come from repeating what others have said—it comes from allowing truth to *land* in you. Not just intellectually, but energetically.

Knowledge is inherited. Wisdom is *embodied*.

Knowledge is something you carry. Wisdom is something that carries *you*.

And you'll know you've touched wisdom not because you can explain it, but because it changes how you live— how you speak, how you choose, how you show up when no one is watching.

It doesn't shout. It resonates. It doesn't demand to be right. It simply *feels* true.

The Two Paths: Reaction or Resilience

---

*"Some things are beyond human comprehension
and must be trickled down from the higher realms
at a level and volume consistent with your
spiritual maturation."*
— Spirit World

Your soul was not built to break—it was built to rise.

She shares with us that life offers two primary responses:

You can live in *reaction,* or you can live in *resilience.*

The reactionary soul is easily swayed by conditions. It measures worth by external chaos and seeks control when uncertainty strikes. It escapes through overthinking, indulgence, or defensiveness—because it doesn't yet trust its own power.

But the resilient soul...

It doesn't pretend to be invincible. It feels the ache. It wrestles with grief. But it listens. It lets pain shape insight instead of identity. It doesn't ask, *"Why is this happening to me?"* but rather, *"What is this teaching me about myself?"*

Wisdom doesn't come all at once. It arrives like rain on parched ground—absorbing slowly over time.

When Pain Becomes a Lens

"Anger, my love, is not the enemy—it's a signal. But left unattended, it becomes a storyteller, and not a truthful one." – Spirit World

---

Anger is a messenger, not a compass. Resentment is what happens when the soul forgets its own light.

At its root, resentment is often born from a perceived lack—a lack of justice, of love, of being heard or seen. But when we carry that pain too long, it begins to speak for us. It colors how we see others. It anchors us to the moment we were hurt, even when the moment has long passed.

Spirit put it this way: "You can't keep unpacking your grief into the same old room and expect to feel free. At some point, you must choose a different doorway—the one that allows you to heal and evolve emotionally. Because you can't dwell in pain and walk in peace at the same time."

Spirit doesn't ask you to forget. But it does ask you to stop building your identity around the architecture of your pain.

The Limitations of the Human Mind

The mind is a helpful tool—not a spiritual authority.

It tries to organize life into understandable boxes. But Spirit doesn't live in boxes. It lives in the spaces between them.

The mind is bound by time. By ego. By patterns of avoidance and protection. It relies on logic to stay safe. But wisdom often comes through what *doesn't* make sense at first—through vibration, through subtle knowing, through sacred contradiction.

We must learn to empty our minds of what we think we know, so Spirit can show us something more.

The Value of Context

What feels like a detour may be the design.

From a spiritual perspective, nothing is wasted — not even our pain.

The lost job. The broken relationship. The missed opportunity. These may seem like failures from the mind's perspective. But Spirit sees differently. It sees the long arc. It knows the way heartbreak becomes humility, how delay becomes preparation, how grief stretches the soul so that it may hold more compassion.

The Humility of Not Knowing

Wisdom waits in the quiet.

True wisdom begins the moment we say, *I don't know.*
Not as defeat, but as invitation.

Spirit reminds us: "Wisdom doesn't yell. It whispers. And the quieter you become, the more you'll hear and understand it."

We don't need more certainty. We need more capacity to sit with mystery. The spiritually mature are not the ones with all the answers. They are the ones who can hold the question without trying to force it closed.

Wisdom will find you—if you give it room to enter.

Journaling Prompts

Living in Wisdom

1. Where in my life am I living in reaction rather than resilience?
2. Describe a moment of deep personal growth through adversity. What changed spiritually as a result?

Healing Through Awareness

3. What old stories or hurts still color my present reality?
4. Write a letter to someone or something you're holding resentment toward. Then, write a second letter to yourself from Spirit's point of view. What shifted in the way you think, feel and process this challenge?

The Mind's Limits and Spirit's Lessons

5. When has your mind drawn a conclusion that Spirit later overturned? What did you learn?
6. Share a time when something that looked like failure became a turning point for growth.

Sitting with Mystery

7. What spiritual questions are you carrying now? Can you sit with them without demanding a resolution?

8. In what ways can you become a clearer vessel for wisdom in your everyday life?

A Final Reflection

Wisdom does not rush. It does not shout. It does not chase.

It moves like breath—subtle, rhythmic, and always near.

To live wisely is not to collect more answers, but to become more available to them. It is not to speak with certainty, but to carry your questions like sacred seeds.

She offers a different perspective to the spiritually minded, "Let the world chase knowledge, while you quietly invite wisdom."

And when you do, wisdom will come. Softly. Faithfully. In its own divine time.

CHAPTER 7 – THE MATURITY OF MANIFESTATION: LETTING GO, READINESS, AND TRUSTING DIVINE TIMING

"Manifestation is not a performance of positivity. It is a quiet becoming. You don't attract what you want—you attract what you're ready to steward."
– Spirit World

We often think of manifestation as something we *do* - something to master or execute with precision. But Spirit offered a gentler view. Manifestation, she said, is less about effort and more about evolution. It isn't the result of saying the right words at the right moon phase. It's about whether your energy, your life, your heart are spacious enough to receive what you think you're calling in.

True manifestation, then, reflects spiritual maturity. It is not hurried. It does not grasp. It listens. It lets go. It trusts the invisible threads being woven behind the scenes.

Desire Versus Readiness: Why Some Dreams Are Delayed—And Why That's a Gift

---

"Spirit waits for readiness, not rhetoric."
— Spirit World

In modern spiritual circles, manifestation has been reduced to a checklist:

- Make a vision board
- Say your affirmations
- Set your intentions

Yet she reminds us, "Spirit isn't your delivery service, my love. It's your partner."

You may desire a loving partnership, but are you emotionally available? You may wish for abundance, but do you trust life to support you? You may dream of awakening, but are you willing to release control?

Spirit doesn't respond to want. It responds to resonance. The more you become the vibration of what you seek, the closer it draws.

Letting Go to Let in: Becoming A Clearer Vessel for What's to Come

Manifestation isn't just about calling in the new. It's also about clearing out the old.

We often say we want change while clinging to the very patterns that block it. We hold tight to identities we've outgrown. We stay in relationships that drain us. We resist the space that transformation requires.

Spirit says, "You can't plant something new in a garden you've refused to weed."

Letting go is sacred preparation. It is not loss. It is alignment. It's the soul making room for what is sacred, timely, and true.

The Mystery of Divine Timing: *Why Delay Is Not Denial*

"What is meant for you cannot be late," she said.
Only lovingly delayed."
— Spirit World

From where we stand, delays feel unfair. But from Spirit's vantage, timing is orchestration, as there are unseen conditions that must ripen before something is ready to bloom.

Sometimes manifestation is being prepared on multiple levels:

- Your emotional nervous system is anchoring in stability.
- Another person's healing is required for your paths to align.
- Divine grace is creating synchronicity that can't be rushed.

Manifestation Is Not a Spell—It's a State

It is becoming the energy you seek. It's not about visualizing harder. It's about living softer.

If you want to receive something generous, live generously. If you long for peace, cultivate internal spaciousness. If you seek spiritual partnership, show up as one.

You become the living altar. A space where Spirit feels welcome.

The Maturity of Not Knowing: Why Trust Is the Highest Form of Manifestation

Those walking in spiritual maturity don't beg the universe for shortcuts.

They hold space for mystery. They surrender their timelines. They trust that Spirit is always at work—even when it's quiet.

"Trust, my darling, is the highest form of co-creation," She shared.

Journaling Prompts

Desire & Readiness

1. What is one desire I hold that may require a personal shift before it can arrive?
2. What might readiness look like—emotionally, spiritually, or practically?
3. Where am I still trying to control what I'm meant to trust?

Letting Go to Let In

4. What am I still holding onto that might be blocking what I've asked for?
5. How can I gently begin to release it—mentally, emotionally, or physically?

Trusting the Timing

6. Write about a past delay that turned out to be a blessing in hindsight.
7. What parts of me are still unfolding in preparation for what I've called in?

Living as a Vessel

8. What small daily action aligns with the future I envision?
9. How can I begin living as though my manifestation is already here?

10. What would deepen in me if I allowed manifestation to be a process of becoming rather than acquiring?

A Final Reflection

Manifestation is not a magic trick. It is a mirror. It reflects not just what you want, but who you are becoming.

Spirit does not operate on urgency. It flows through openness. The moment you release your grip is the moment grace begins its work. What you seek is not far off—it's forming within you.

Let it arrive on sacred terms. Let it find you available.

CHAPTER 8 – ALIGNMENT AND REMEMBRANCE: WHY WE FORGET WHO WE ARE— AND HOW TO COME BACK

"The human condition is primarily about alignment and remembrance. We are not here to achieve. We are here to remember." – Spirit World

There comes a point in the soul's journey when the striving begins to quiet, and something softer calls us home. The illusions we once chased begin to lose their shine, and what once felt urgent now feels irrelevant. We begin to sense that the essence of who we are was never gone—only buried beneath the noise, the roles, and the proving. The invitation is to return. Not to who we were, but to who we've always been.

We forget for a time, caught in the performance of becoming. But as remembrance returns, so does peace. We shed what isn't ours, speak more gently, listen more deeply. We reclaim joy not as a luxury, but as a compass pointing us back to soul. And in doing so, we begin to embody something richer—not for show, but for wholeness.

A Journey of Sacred Forgetting

Most of us don't realize we've drifted from our true self until something startles and reawakens us—a loss, an illness, a sorrow.

Spirit calls this "sacred amnesia" - the soul deliberately forgetting who we are. Not as punishment, but as preparation. It forgets its light so it can rediscover it with reverence. The forgetting allows us to move through the grit of human life, collecting experience, feeling contrast, experiencing illusion.

"We make personalities out of pain and identities out of survival," she'd say, "And then wonder why we feel unrest."

The first half of life often becomes a devotion to performance—chasing careers, validation, partnerships, and polished narratives. But for the soul, it's all just scaffolding to help us reach more elevated state.

The Second Half: When We Begin to Realign

The turning point is quiet. There's no parade. No spiritual certificate. Just a growing sense of dissatisfaction with what once impressed us. We crave depth, not noise. Simplicity, not spectacle.

"When the outer self and the inner self are congruent," Spirit said, "we experience peace—even if our circumstances still need adjusting."

We begin to choose what nourishes us rather than what performs well.

We clear out what isn't ours.

And slowly, gently, joy returns. Not a loud, performative joy—but a quiet gladness in being who we are, where we are.

Joy as a Compass

Spirit said, "If you want joy, you must stop watching life from the sidelines. Joy requires participation."

We think we're tired. But more often, we're disembodied.

We confuse busyness with purpose, distraction with connection. We scroll more than we sit. We ache for intimacy but run from presence. But the soul craves engagement—not achievement. Real joy is simple and sacred.

Joy is sitting on the porch, laughing with a neighbor. Joy is hearing your favorite song and singing out loud. Joy is handing someone a cup of tea and enjoying a deep conversation.

"You're not too old, too quirky, too burnt out," Spirit said. "You're just too stuck. And stuckness is not a life sentence—it's a signal that something richer is calling."

A Message for Women: Returning to Your Own Soul

"If you were raised on scarcity, you'll chase security," Spirit said. "But security without growth is not safety. It's stagnation."

Many women enter relationships before fully knowing themselves. We confuse attachment with safety. We build a home in someone else's dreams—and then wonder why we feel unseen in our own.

As women, we must reclaim a spiritual interior life that isn't dependent on partnership, roles, or titles. Without it, we hover beneath the surface of our true potential.

Being married isn't the problem. Being unclaimed by your own soul is.

"Your soul does not envy another's path," she reminds us. "It mourns the one you refuse to walk."

A Message for Men: Provision Isn't Presence

> *"You are not less of a man for being emotionally and spiritually present. You are more of a soul for allowing yourself to evolve."* – *Spirit World*

"Many men mistake financial wealth for wholeness and completion," Spirit said. "But a full bank account doesn't mean a full soul."

Provision can tether one to a performance-based life where titles become a sort of trap. And when men equate worth with output, they risk becoming strangers to their emotional and spiritual selves.

"Don't let your abundance become your prison," she warned. "A man can be the provider of a home and still feel homeless within himself."

True masculinity has so much more depth and so many more layers, but it requires courage to be curious, self-reflective and emotionally present.

Turning Wisdom Into Offering

The final chapter of our human journey isn't about success—it's about spiritual embodiment. It's not about legacy—it's about presence.

We stop striving. We start showing up. We stop talking. We start resonating. We become nourishment—for ourselves, and for those around us.

We remember who we are.

And in doing so, we become a living invitation for others to remember too.

Journaling Prompts

Alignment & Identity

1. Where in my life am I living to impress rather than to express?
2. What did I once believe made me worthy that no longer feels true?
3. What roles or inherited beliefs have shaped my life that are asking to be released?

The Call of Joy

4. When was the last time I felt true, unfiltered joy?
5. What simple joy can I say yes to this week?
6. Have I mistaken busyness for purpose? What might shift if I chose presence?

For Women

7. In what ways have I postponed or minimized my own voice to support another's?
8. What does it mean to be claimed by my own soul?

For Men

9. How have I used provision to define my worth?
10. What part of my emotional or spiritual self longs to be expressed?

A Final Reflection

We forget who we are—not because we are broken, but because the demands of the outer world are noisy.

The soul is patient. And when we stop long enough to listen, we can feel its presence.

The soul doesn't disappear. It waits for the moment you listen and starts leading you home.

CHAPTER 9 – HUMILITY, ABUNDANCE, AND SACRED SERVICE

"I cannot impress upon you more the importance of being humble. Humbleness flows from gratitude and thoughtfulness."
– Spirit World

There was something grounded and profoundly human in what She shared on this morning. It wasn't grand. It wasn't mystical. It was beautifully ordinary. Her voice, gentle but firm, reminded us that spiritual evolution doesn't always roar—it often whispers through the smallest acts of care. While the world hurries to be seen and celebrated, Spirit pointed to something quieter: presence. To live humbly, she said, is to walk as if the ground itself is holy and to treat others as if they are, too. While spiritual gifts may sparkle, it is grace that truly shines. True maturity does not draw attention to itself—it draws others inward, back to their own truth, their own divinity. It asks nothing in return. And yet, its impact is lasting.

Spiritual Success Is Rooted in Service

"The more successful you are, the more
conscientious you must be."
— Spirit World

She spoke with conviction about what it means to hold power and influence with integrity. If you've experienced abundance, you must share it. If you've known joy, you must offer it.

Abundance is not a status symbol. It is a responsibility.

This doesn't mean over-giving or becoming a spiritual martyr. It means staying connected to humanity, remembering that your elevation was never meant to isolate you—it was meant to give you reach. And through that reach, you plant seeds of healing, kindness, and wisdom.

True spiritual success isn't loud. It's not measured in platforms or applause. It's measured in presence—the subtle but unmistakable shift your energy leaves in a room.

The Sacredness of Simple Gestures

Spirit reminisced about a time in history when connection was slower, more intentional:

- Writing a thank-you card by hand
- Baking something for a neighbor who is struggling with grief and loss
- Calling someone not to fix or solve anything, but simply to be present
- Spending time in unrushed, soul-to-soul conversation

These acts may seem small, but their vibrational signature is enormous. They stitch love into the world in invisible ways.

When we bypass these opportunities for connection in pursuit of status, speed, or surface validation, we fall out of alignment with Spirit. We begin to crave applause over authenticity. We chase impact over intimacy. And when we detach from our spiritual essence, we lose our clearest channel with what makes us divine and richly satisfied.

Ego, Performance, and the Illusion of Importance

"You must learn to be powerful without the proof," She impressed, "and generous without the guarantee of recognition."

Humility isn't weakness. It's spirituality in its highest form and the soul's way of remembering the origin of its power.

When ego drives our service, we begin to mistake performance for purpose. We show up only when we're praised. We give only when we're recognized. We begin to fear invisibility and irrelevance.

Yet, She reminds us invisibility is often where Spirit works best.

Sometimes, Spirit will tuck you away—not to punish you, but to preserve you. To mature your gifts. To refine your energy. To prepare your soul for deeper levels of sacred work that require no spotlight to be effective.

The Energetics of Humble Service

When we move through the world humbly—grounded in spiritual presence rather than personal ego—our energy changes:

- We don't need to compete, because we trust divine timing.
- We don't need to defend, because we lead with grace.
- We don't need to over-give, because our worth isn't measured by exhaustion.
- We don't need to control, because we've surrendered the outcome to something wiser than us.

Humble service is magnetic. It draws in exactly who and what is meant for us—not because we demanded it, but because we became the version of ourselves ready to receive it.

Sacred Living in Ordinary Moments

We do not need to work outside our current capacity to be of service. We simply need to be available. There is power in sacred participation—the daily acts of intention that no one ever witnesses, but Spirit sees.

Spirit called these types of gestures our soul's true credentials.

- Sending a blessing to a client, neighbor or friend with a silent prayer
- Leaving flowers for someone you may not know well
- Listening—really listening—to someone who is unraveling
- Sending words of encouragement to a person who is struggling

Each action is an echo in the spirit world, a thread in the collective weave of grace.

Journaling Prompts

1. Where in my life do I confuse visibility with value? How might I shift my focus from being seen to being of service?
2. In what ways can I practice spiritual humility without diminishing my worth? How does humility serve to strengthen my leadership?
3. What simple, thoughtful gesture could I offer this week as sacred service? Is there someone I feel called to support?
4. Have I ever been healed by helping another? What did that experience teach me about energy, exchange, and grace?
5. What part of me craves recognition more than resonance? How can I soften that part with compassion and redirect it toward service?
6. When was I most spiritually generous without anyone knowing? What did it awaken in me?
7. How do I define spiritual success—and does that definition feel aligned with my soul's values?

Final Reflection: Let Your Grace Be Contagious

"Those most in tune with Spirit rarely speak the loudest. But their grace echoes long after they've left the room." – Spirit World

---

Spiritual evolution is not a badge. It's a presence. A tone in your voice. A quiet way of moving through the world.

It's the way you speak to the weary. The way you bless a moment without saying a word. The way you leave someone else better—because you remembered who you are.

Let your grace be contagious. Let your kindness ripple through the unseen realms.

INTERLUDE – THE SOUL OF LEADERSHIP: HOLDING THE LIGHT FOR THE COLLECTIVE

"True leadership is measured not by what you achieve—but by how deeply your presence invites others to remember their own light."
– Spirit World

There comes a point in every soul's journey where you must ask yourself—not what position you hold, but what vibration you lead from. You see, being a leader has little to do with titles or influence in the worldly sense. True leadership is spiritual stewardship. It requires that you keep just enough distance—emotionally, mentally, even socially—to hear your Higher Self clearly above the crowd.

This is not detachment in the cold sense. It's a sacred space of clarity, so you're not swept into the tides of ego—wanting to be liked, included, or applauded. Those things, my love, will dull your compass, she noted.

You cannot afford to climb so high in your own self-importance that you lose vision in the fog. But neither can you let yourself get tangled in the thorns at the bottom—

pricked by the need to please, or poisoned by judgment, fear, and noise.

Leadership is about seeing the whole, not aligning too closely with any single interest or voice—especially if that voice begins to speak louder than your own intuition. If your lens is clouded by allegiance, then your decisions will reflect bias, not wisdom. And your task, precious one, is to hold the light for the entire group—especially those whose voices have been quieted by fear, inequity, or pain.

Make no mistake, if you walk this path of spiritual leadership, you will be tested. There will be whispers behind doors, baited provocations, and moments where your truth is challenged publicly and privately. But this is not a punishment—it's a revealing. It shows you which voice is louder within: the one born of shadow, or the one born of light.

So choose. Not just once, but daily.

Whether your leadership is formal or unseen, whether it shows up in boardrooms or at the family table, you must be mindful of the voices in your head. Whose tone dominates your thoughts? Do they speak of compromise or clarity? Of duty or distraction?

You cannot serve as a true leader if you're too identified with one group, one need, one side. It muffles your own soul's signal.

Now, don't mistake me—leadership need not be lonely. You don't need to retreat to the mountains to find your truth. But you do need relationships that exist outside your roles. You need people who see you, not your title. People who challenge you not because of your clout, but because they love you enough to call your soul forward.

That's where your strength is renewed. That's where the leader and the human meet—in the quiet grace of circles where your only role is to be whole.

The Whole Is Greater Than the Sum of Its Parts

"You must understand, my love, that in spiritual leadership, you are not simply managing people — you are stewarding energy. You are tending to a collective soul. And within that sacred container, every vibration matters."
— Spirit World

There is a tendency, especially among the heart-led and service-driven, to try and hold everything together — even when it frays. To keep saying yes, when the soul is crying no. But hear her clearly:

"The whole is always greater than the sum of its parts. Which means the integrity of the collective must, at times, take precedence over any one relationship, role, or responsibility that threatens its harmony."

Every spiritual leader has the right to peace. To clarity. To a clean field.

You have the right — and the responsibility — to be free of emotional turmoil and conflict. Not because you lack compassion, but because conflict clouds the channel. It drains the very life force needed to serve.

When someone within your circle — be it a client, partner, or team member — consistently introduces manipulation, control, or emotional distortion, it is not spiritual to "stay and fix." It is wise to step back and see.

Sometimes the most spiritual act is the most human one: drawing a boundary, pulling the cord, and walking away with love.

"You must not carry what is not yours," she said. "You must not spend your sacred energy trying to appease someone whose pattern is rooted in their own unhealed pain—especially when that pain begins to shape your path, cloud your vision, or fracture your peace."

Do not underestimate the burden of attachment.

"I've seen many a good soul entangled in emotional obligation, thinking it noble to stay, to compromise, to tolerate. But let me say this as clearly as I can: If the weight of that attachment begins to silence your voice, dull your joy, or take your work off course—it is too high a price."

You are not here to carry others across the threshold by force. You are here to hold the door open for those who are ready—and to keep the light burning for those who are not.

So, love them from afar if you must. Bless their path. And then come back to yours—clean, clear, and ready.

Because when you serve from alignment, not appeasement, your work becomes the greater sum. It moves mountains. It restores hearts. It transforms lives.

"And that, my darling," Spirit said, "is the real leadership of the soul."

When the Leak Is the Lesson

---

*"You are not here to walk behind someone,
cleaning up their messes. Your job is to lead. Not
to chase, not to explain, not to defend. To lead."*
– Spirit World

There are those who sow confusion with intent. They stir unrest not from unawareness, but from habit—gossiping behind closed doors, sharing fragments of truth to discredit others, or lashing out when confronted with boundaries.

"There are some, she shared, who do not know how to feel powerful unless they're dismantling someone else's peace."

These individuals thrive in distortion. They do not seek healing—they seek control.

"They'll tell just enough truth to make the lie believable," she said, "but never enough to reveal their own shadow."

It is tempting for the heart-centered leader to try and correct the narrative, defend their name, or pour energy into repairing the damage. But this is a trap.

"Every time you try to plug the leak, she said, "another one appears. Because the problem is not the hole—it's the source."

These souls do not want resolution. They want reaction. And the more you invest in cleanup, the more power they draw from your energy field. It is a siphoning of sacred resources, cloaked as spiritual concern.

There is no peace in appeasement. There is no service in self-sacrifice. And there is no clarity in dancing around someone else's chaos.

Sacred Leadership Is Discernment in Action

"The whole is greater than the sum of its parts.
And if a single part is rotting the whole, the soul of
the work suffers." — Spirit World

Spiritual maturity means knowing when to stay soft, and
when to stand firm. It means choosing truth even when
it's not popular. It means protecting the field you've been
entrusted with—even if it means saying goodbye to
someone who's not ready to walk in integrity.

You are not called to manage dysfunction. You are called
to embody light. And sometimes, the only way to do that
is to walk away from the noise and let your peace speak
for you.

Journal Prompts for Sacred Reflection

Let these questions guide you inward. There's no need to rush. The answers may rise slowly, like morning light through fog:

Inner Inventory

1. Where in my leadership or life have I chosen to keep the peace rather than be at peace?
2. Who in my life currently uses confusion, gossip, or emotional chaos to gain control? How does this impact my clarity?
3. Have I been pouring energy into someone or something that continually leaks or drains my spirit? Why?

Releasing the Ego

4. What part of me still believes I must rescue or fix others to be seen as loving or spiritual?
5. What would it feel like to let go of that role? To let people have their perceptions and trust Spirit to hold the truth?
6. Where am I being called to soften—and where am I being called to stand firm?

Spiritual Responsibility

7. What simple act of kindness can I offer this week that reconnects me to sacred service in a heartfelt, human way?

Final Whisper from Spirit

Leadership, in the highest sense, is never about commanding others. It is about becoming so steady in your own alignment that others remember what alignment feels like.

It is not loud. It is luminous.

You are not here to be a savior. You are here to be a signal.

Keep your frequency clear.

Let your leadership be love in action.

And remember: The most powerful light is the one that quietly holds the room—even after it has left.

CHAPTER 10 – THE ALCHEMY OF LOSS: HOW PAIN RESTORES THE SOUL'S INTEGRITY

"Through pain, the soul is rerouted—not away, but back to what is essential."
— Spirit World

Loss is the great equalizer. It levels our illusions, dismantles our defenses, and lays bare the raw truth of who we are and what we value.

But loss is also a great alchemist. When honored as sacred, it transforms what was fractured into something more whole.

In many spirit-led conversations, Her presence emphasized that grief is not a diversion from the path—it is part of the path. Through channeled guidance, she reminds us that pain is not a failure, but an invitation.

Pain as a Sacred Teacher

"Emotional pain is the soul whispering. Physical pain is what happens when you ignore the whisper for too long." – Spirit World

---

The initial response to pain is almost always resistance.

We tense, withdraw, distract, or deny.

From the perspective of the ego, pain is punishment.

But from the soul's view, pain is a compass.

She, in spirit, helps convey that physical and emotional pain are not separate phenomena but echoes of the same frequency at different intensities. Physical pain is the magnification of unacknowledged emotional pain.

Rigid thinking, self-neglect, and the need to control what cannot be controlled often show up through the body as tension, fatigue, or chronic issues.

Not as punishment—but as communication.

Healing begins not when we resist pain, but when we soften toward it. And pain is not your punishment. It's your turning point.

The Invitation to Be Vulnerable

> *"Let your pain speak, but don't let it steer. Let your sorrow breathe but not build a home in your heart."* — *Spirit World*

Pain asks us to turn inward—not in collapse, but in softness.

True vulnerability is not about emotional exposure without boundaries. It is the sacred willingness to feel deeply without explanation, defense, or urgency to fix.

Pain helps reveal where we've veered from our spiritual center:

- Overgiving from depletion, not devotion
- Withholding from fear, not discernment
- Controlling instead of allowing
- Distrusting instead of receiving

We often bounce between extremes—numbing or over-functioning. But the soul seeks presence, not performance.

The Energetic Reset of the Soul

"Some lessons must be learned in the dark, because only in shadow does the soul remember its own light." — Spirit World

In spiritual terms, pain is a recalibration.

It brings us home to ourselves.

When grief is fully felt—not bypassed or buried—it becomes a cleansing force. It draws out what we've ignored and gently dissolves what no longer belongs.

This isn't divine punishment. It's purification.

Pain doesn't always heal with time—but it is transformed by devotion, attention, and presence.

When You Want to Disappear: A Channeled Message for the Tender Moments

---

"The mark of a true spiritual leader isn't how brightly they shine when celebrated, but how gently they walk when misunderstood."
— Spirit World

My darling, when someone has lashed out—through words or energy—you may feel the instinct to disappear. To shrink. To slip beneath the surface where no one can find you.

That's human. It's the tender part of you trying to protect itself. But you must not stay there.

There is great strength in choosing to rise—not despite the wound, but with it. Not as a victim wearing pain like a costume, but as a soul who has turned it into wisdom.

When those moments arrive, call in your soul tribe—not as cheerleaders, but as a loving current around you. A quiet strength beneath your flame.

Being a medium is not comfortable, my love. It was never meant to be.

You were chosen because you agreed to feel.

Not to fit in. Not to be praised. But to stand in the in-between spaces and hold the light.

You are not here to disappear. You are here to be seen—and to help others feel seen, too.

The Return to Integrity

---

*"Spiritual maturity isn't the absence of pain. It's
knowing how to bow to it with grace."*
– Spirit World

The root of integrity is integer—meaning whole.

Loss, when honored, doesn't destroy us. It reveals us.

It rearranges our lives with more authenticity:

- Less performance, more presence
- Less proving, more peace
- Less striving, more surrender

We begin to live not as someone trying to *become*
something—but as someone remembering who they
already are.

Journaling Prompts

Your Body as Messenger

1. What physical tension or discomfort has been speaking to you?
2. Is there an emotional or spiritual message underneath it?
3. What part of your life is asking for softness instead of strategy?
4. What would it look like to respond with compassion rather than control?

Grief as Alchemy

5. What personal loss reshaped your soul's priorities?
6. What have you learned through pain that no other path could have taught?
7. Where can you let grief clarify instead of causing you to collapse?

The Soul's Tender Return

8. When have you wanted to disappear emotionally or spiritually?
9. What does it mean to "bow to pain with grace" in your own life?

The Strength of Being Seen

10. How does your heart respond to the idea that you're here to be seen?

11. What part of you still hides?
12. How might your presence become a refuge for someone else?

A Final Reflection: What Remains

"Grief is love with no place to go. It aches like unrequited love. But the soul doesn't disappear—it expands. And when you remember that, your love still lands. It is received, held, and returned—in the quiet spaces, in the soft presence of the infinite." – Spirit World

---

What we grieve most deeply often reflects what we loved most truly.

Love, when anchored in the soul, does not end with death or absence—it deepens.

Let loss do its holy work. Let it cleanse, clarify, and reorient—not just toward healing, but toward truth.

In the stillness that follows sorrow, something sacred emerges:

A deeper softness.

A wider knowing.

A more soul-aligned you.

Grief will not leave you empty. It will leave you honest.

ACKNOWLEDGEMENT

I dedicate this book to the female soul whose earthly presence I never had the privilege of knowing, yet whose companionship from the invisible realm has become one of the most profound guiding forces in my life. Her presence from the spirit world arrived with such precision and grace which felt less like a meeting and more like a remembering. The comfort she offered, the timing of her messages, and the sacred rhythm of her teachings have awakened places in my soul that language alone could never reach.

What I've come to understand about this teacher in Spirit is that she is, above all, a visionary. From the very beginning of our work together, I sensed that what we were co-creating extended far beyond the pages of this book. Her wisdom was to ripple outward into the hearts, hands, and voices of other spiritual teachers, seekers, and leaders to raise the collective frequency of this planet.

This is not a manual, nor a method. It is a consecrated space, crafted for those who lead from the soul's deep well. A quiet invitation to stop searching, to begin listening, and to trust the divine self as a living, luminous truth. It calls us back to humility, presence, and devotion. For those who feel called to carry the teachings from this book into workshops, retreats, and spiritual circles, you are joining a movement—a quiet revolution of remembrance and realignment.

Unlike traditional titles on channeling or spiritual growth, these teachings weaves together mediumship, spiritual psychology, and grounded daily devotion—channeled through the steady, familiar voice of one of the most respected figures in contemporary mediumship.

ABOUT THE AUTHOR

Amy Marohn

Amy Marohn is the owner of Sensorium Hypnosis located in Lake Stevens, WA. She offers in-person and virtual sessions across the globe weaving spiritual coaching, mediumship and metaphysical healing into her work. She also hosts spiritual workshops to provide clients with more opportunities for personal growth and social connection.

A lifelong battle with rare and chronic illness inspired in her a desire to help underserved populations access better healthcare, education and work opportunities. For several decades she worked in the field of rehabilitation, health care public policy and nonprofit management until a near-death experience revealed her current path. Amy has a bachelor's degree in metaphysical science, a master's degree in rehabilitation counseling and a master hypnotist certification. She is also an ordained metaphysical minister through the International Metaphysical Ministry.

You can learn more or connect with Amy online at www.sensoriumhypnosis.com. There you will find spiritual blogs, a scheduling link to explore one-to-one sessions and her Spotify podcast, Healer Within.

Would you like to use this book and the corresponding journal, *The Whispers Within*, for retreats, book clubs, or spiritual workshops? Visit me online to explore licensure and training opportunities.

www.ingramcontent.com/pod-product-compliance
Lightning Source LLC
Chambersburg PA
CBHW060631130626
46555CB00002B/751